THE HUNTERS IN THE SNOW

THE HUNTERS IN THE SNOW

DOUGLAS HOUSTON

BLOODAXE BOOKS

ISBN: 1 85224 265 5

First published 1994 by
Bloodaxe Books Ltd,
P.O. Box 1SN,
Newcastle upon Tyne NE99 1SN.

Bloodaxe Books Ltd acknowledges
the financial assistance of Northern Arts.

Cover printing by J. Thomson Colour Printers Ltd, Glasgow.

Printed in Great Britain by
Cromwell Press Ltd, Broughton Gifford, Melksham, Wiltshire.

To my mother,
Mary Elizabeth Houston

Acknowledgements

Acknowledgements are due to the editors of the following publications in which some of these poems first appeared: *Aber Writing, Bête Noire, The Honest Ulsterman, Jacaranda Review* (USA), *New Welsh Review, Planet, Poetry Book Society Anthology 1987-1988* (PBS/Hutchinson, 1988), *Poetry Review, Poetry Wales,* and *Slightly Soiled.* Earlier versions of certain poems appeared in Meic Stephens's anthology, *The Bright Field* (Carcanet Press, 1991).

Thanks are due to the Welsh Arts Council for a writer's bursary awarded in 1990-91.

Contents

THE BOOK OF SHACKLETON

Song of the Cuckoo

His courts are buoyant with the gentle breathing
Of green upholstery inundating hillsides,
For leaves are his very favourite,
And his prayer to himself is always
To make the world an inside-out lung.
Each year the May offensive's launched
With pollens and evaporating saps
Deranging what constrains the blood,
Potentiating gender scents
To force hallucinatory shifts
In purpose and priority;
The cities rally with rain
And civilisation remembers itself
Every time the barometer falls.

He is the archetype of all whom power
And wealth in such lavish concentrations
Have forced, unhinged, into queer cul-de-sacs,
This mad divinity unshakeably persuaded
That he's a wooden toy artfully contrived
So any drift of air goes up his flue
To sound cu – koo, cu – koo, cu – koo.
When I shot the cuckoo I knew myself blessed
By his adversary who fits us strait for winter,
And my gaze reassumed the rock's blank rigour.

Passage

Settled as fine dew on the waxy leaves
And wearing the sheen in the rarest lead ore,
The angel was in the rhododendron thicket
That's spreading across the disused mine's sprawl.
Down gaps in high ridges, the sun, still pale,
Vaporised grave-mould furring the mountains,
But the road took me further, up into winter,
Grey oxides on everything, air, vegetation,
The moment gone, the resurrection over,
And all the dead back at their pleasures,
Wherever they'd found their excellent silences,
Where the rhythms of action vibrated as music,
And their eyes twinkled, and they were changed.

W.H. Auden in Cwmbrwyno

(for Bruce Woodcock)

Since to discount the hereafter as a possibility
        Seemed at best rather unfeasible,
At worst irredeemable folly (though to imagine it
        Remained a poser limestone half solved),
It hardly amazes me, who became inured to surprise,
        To come to consciousness up here.
Indeed, I am delighted at whatever dispensation
        Has placed me amid this landscape
Like a locality I loved. Though the machines are gone,
        The derelict wheelpits, grey spoil-heaps,
And several crumbled buildings linked by the purposive stream
        Announce *lead-mine* to one informed
In these matters from infancy. To me such uplands spoke
        A code of love it took a life
To render into simple language of reciprocation:
        I held their desolation dear,
And their complete abandonment always made room for me,
        Whether the barren *Ding an Sich*,
Or in the privacy of space entered through memory's adit.
        The after-life advantages
The visitor, it appears. No guide book is necessary now
        The mood of place translates itself
Into particulars of what happened here – mostly labour;
        The delve and drainage, sorting rock,
Clean ore sent clattering seawards along the little railway,
        While, out of sight, a fortune grew,
Then faltered till silence took root in 1888.
        These hills do not care to impress,
Ancient and scraggy with ribs of stone breaking through the thin green
        So slowly healing the mine's scar
(And certainly not interested in my sympathy
        In their dedolant emptiness).
Only the bones of sheep might be considered additions
        To what the paid-off miners left;
Beyond loss, what remains long since utility collapsed
        To irreducible aesthetics
Of rusted curves of rail, dejected masonry and peace,
        Is absolute to me, resisting

Even the colonisation of the imagination
        And silently insisting on
Its terms of barefaced honesty beyond alternatives.
        Though its poetic forms appealed
(Intimidatingly complex), Wales meant little to me
        After the early photographs,
Memorialising how at six I loved simple machines
        On holiday in Rhayader.
Here, however, I'm at home below the slouching mountains' mist,
        Donated random mineral finds
Turned over by my foot – this algae fossilised on slate,
        A slow subaqueous holograph
Whose text is years in millions. Shattering a weighty chunk of rock
        Against an unyielding boulder
Has introduced to daylight a good vein of galena
        Whose lustrous facets quite outshine
The subservient metal wept by these fractile crystals
        When smelting rends their bond with sulphur....
From what I gather, the Great Powers have not mended their ways,
        Monied, immune, even more dangerous
In uncontainable Megalopolis, since foreclosure
        Deprived me of my mortal manor;
But to my list of sites least likely to be further robbed
        This nook some way below Plynlimon
Is added to become one of the irrefutable Prophets.

Slate City

Sun, and the thick pelt of slate-shards
On hillsides is softly lustrous,
Attractively indigenous
Aesthetic of devastation,
Baffling attempted estimation
Of how many hand-sized fragments
Of laminae so thoroughly
Bury original contours.

Though mostly abundant rubble,
From bits trodden in roadside grass
To spoil-heaps years of shifts amassed,
A disembowelled topography
Of slate's blue-grey ubiquity,
The sheen of regimented roofs
Exemplifies the stock-in-trade,
And for municipal ornament

A jagged chunk's set in a square;
Huge tablets are incised with signs
Directing tourists to the mines;
At 'The World's Largest…' levels hacked
Into a looming hill are stacked
In circular diminishments
Like some crude Welsh attempt to raise
A replica stepped pyramid.

Orange with rust, defunct machines,
Discarded narrow-gauge rails, skulls
Of ruined winding sheds annul
The flimsy order superimposed
By the visitors' route: the cafe's closed;
Y Siop, a tart in bright-green paint,
Stands proffering hand-crafted slate,
Looks rather sadly out of place.

Though near retirement, industry
Continues down a potholed track
Where a yard's filled with batched slates packed
In open crates, broken ones piled
To add their tittle to the spoil.
Far into dusk, the sky's subdued
To near the hue of the mineral sprawl,
Night falling like a weightless slab of slate.

ON THE HILL

Pumlumon Fawr

Nothing but snow as the long gradient
Dissolves into thickening mist ahead,
Annulling possible horizons.
Lower down the wind was forming razors
Of ice on stalks of grass and rushes
Coming through the frozen bog's white crust.
Now detail and distinction persist
Only in noting how far each step
Sinks its green boot in unbroken snow.
Trudging through oblivion, my moustache
Stiff with rime, the afternoon becomes
A block where slow deliberation
Hews an urgent text on survival,
A desperate theory built on the hope
That my compass knows what it's doing.

On Snowdon

The start is forty minutes over
Half-dried peat-mires, striated rock-beds,
Always the random assemblies of boulders,
Till a rest, the rucksack dumped
On scant grass with the flesh reduced
To requisitioning oxygen,
Thought pleased as gasps suffice
With its reflection in the empty sky.
The near horizontal is the clack of stones
Shattered by sons investigating force,
And a sheep complaining is distance ahead.
The apex of each breath anticipates
The summit, while I sketch a ramshackle proof
Of the spirit, the sole imperishable,
Merely deformable, though photographs
At three thousand feet postpone
The wasting of the mortal image
At seven years, ten, and forty-three,
Posed beside crags in streaming mist.

A Night Out

Two thousand feet above the torrent's clattering sibilance,
   Past scrambling on heather lost in mist
   Till sharp castellations of boot-prints in peat
   Repeatedly signalled the track's assurance,
Reaching the summit is a spirited trudge through cloud,

An effort in faith, with daylight's rapid fading
   Insistent on its irrevocable deadline,
   With all views down a grey obliteration
   And craggy desolation fading yards ahead,
Faith that the refuge on the top actually exists,

That there will, indeed, be a top, that this eeriness
   Of stones stained with luminescent green lichen
   Constantly nodding out of the blown mist
   Is not some interminable last landscape
With no interest in ever being interesting.

Then a dim taking-shape out on the edge of sight
   Solidifies into a squat stone building,
   Its dirty wired windows filling with night
   While a rising gale roughs up the sky
And vodka slops by torchlight into an old tin mug.

Eryri

After an hour all movement's in tune,
A rhythmic tacking progress uphill
Sprung on economies of muscle
Selecting angles, steady boulders,
Scanning the ways that make the going
Easiest between the quarter-mile rests.

Above the little lake looking back
It's clear the past has not come this far;
Effort's dismantled the routine moods,
Space takes over the sensorium,
And a tricky passage over slabs
Pins all importance to the moment.

Snow still in hollows tinctures the breeze
Drying the path to a stony ochre.
Lazy phrases from a saxophone
Crossing the mile of air between peaks
Are audible when rests ease gasping
On the trudge along this rising ridge.

Thin murmur of cold water
Drawing the afternoon on
Through endless variations
On stone – acres of pebbles,
Amassments of scree, daggers
Whose tons jut from the jumble
Of round-shouldered monoliths
Piled to the white quartz terrace
That shocks the eyes in sunlight.

Dusk is down there among fragments of slate,
Scrap iron, gear-boxes gutted and rusting,
Corrugated walls of barns collapsing,
Where they live down improbably narrow roads
And the cuckoo flutes a mutated call.

Exhaustion and darkness, the tent pitched
On a flat bank by a rapid stream
Clattering over rocks between which
Calm passages hold excerpts of sky:
Peace, a music sad with exclusions,
The petty irritants, the broken.

Tryfan and Wigan

That afternoon we climbed from the lake,
Not supposing we'd get very far,
One son not yet seven, his brother just nine,
My self no model of clean living's dividends,
And not equipped like the earnest types
Whose strides deny intimidation.

But postulate a watcher, let it be
My father's ghost out on the black water,
Whose progeny diminish in his sight
Till, straining, he can barely find three specks
In careful file along the northern ridge
Towards the summit's triple pinnacles.

He's lost us now, up on the level hiatus,
The last shoulder where gales exhilarate
Before big rocks pile steeply to the top
Three hundred feet above our decision
To call it triumph enough, turning back to
The vague track falling through the stony waste.

Time to spare for donning the goggles
To split flint warts with the geologist's hammer,
For selecting the whitest fragments of quartz,
In a leisured descent over hard-won ground
Back to the car for a drive into night
And urban horizons infested with lights.

Mountain-wearied, the boys don't wake,
When the quiet place where we camp is raided
By a horn's sudden torrent flooding me from sleep
To face a blinding battery of headlamps –
Precipices on the fringes of cities,
Malice amused that it offers no choice.

Pulling the Boy Up

Rising traverses on rock facing north
Come to a crux where I pull the boy up,
My body wedged to the waist in a cleft
Between a granite flake and the mountain.
Pulling the boy up the stretch I just climbed,
Trusting my big hands tight round his wrists,
Two miles of road down over his shoulder,
Pulling the boy up and he gets stuck
By the feet in a crack he was trying to use
To get himself up to the going on,
Black peat-paste smearing the ankles,
Blood's thundering demands for more air,
Pulling the boy up towards the top
Where sweated warmth disperses in the sky.

Bird Rock

(for Wayne Metcalfe)

A clean wind cold has narrowed blows through
Interstices in the moment's dense weave
And distances the self from what it feels.
On a high rock island stranded inland
By a level meadow that runs to the sea,
A vertical line of sight composes
The next few bars of upward movement,
Sees cormorants idly wheel across the noon.
Going up, it seems the rock agrees to this,
Donates the holds that hold, but still reserves
Prerogatives of looseness, shakey plates,
Thin flakes that will not take the body's weight.

But sometimes nothing does, not cigarettes
Nor their renunciation, not silence
Nor faint oaths, tied to a cold boulder
On a narrow ledge far above common sense
While out in space misgivings squawk
And the future obscures the next cheque.

Froggat Edge

The hollows in the gale shake out their fragments
Of song flung up from where the Methodists camp
Down in the vale whose greenness terminates
Short of the gritstone cliffs.

Such weather's shaped these towering grotesqueries
Whose wrinkled strata profiled on blank skies
Thrust up impassive physiognomies
Blotchy with blackening rust.

The rock decays to quartz and sandstone dirt,
A narrow bouldered beach skirting the climbs,
A base where breath and pulse may stabilise
Before each fresh attempt.

Half way up Green Gut's forty-five foot crack,
Wedged in a corner by hands, feet, and back,
I am's a pure tense in its liberation
From ageing grievances.

The calculations made, a hand's pressed in
A damp stone slot, jams fast just long enough
To get the right foot up on a good block
And earth the trembling limbs.

Later a mirror shows the web of veins
That map the delicate flesh, locate the pain
Surfacing from a pectoral muscle's strain
Through tiredness fathoms deep.

May Day Solo

Night in a gap in the mountains
reaches maximum darkness and clarity,
the woods and the lake receding to black,
the Milky Way a shawl of light
that makes the peaks distinct.

High on the pyramid whose silhouette
is dominating space to the north-east,
small lights move in some resting place,
the sole event in this poised emptiness
preceding sleep and the morning's climb.

I advance early towards the last snow,
a soiled crust in permanent shadow
where the long ridge holds its line to the top,
anxious before this first time out
on the clean spine of the high arête.

Moving up past difficulty and misgivings
I perch near the crest after twenty minutes,
suddenly exposed to the mid-morning sun
that spills on my face to define
the meeting of desire and its object.

Later on the unhurried descent,
I call the path I join holy,
a place where pure water is given,
where my sons and I received the gift
of the need for the mountains born in us.

Looking up where the thin stream unbraids
in its long fall down the black rocks,
I fill my bottle at the flow's own speed
and swallow what has measured itself,
tasting time in unfamiliar newness.

* * *

Neighbours

i.m. Dic Jones, 1913-1987, Llanfihangel-ar-Arth

On the night we moved in you brought mushrooms,
And over the three succeeding years
You proved the good neighbour you seemed then,
Arriving with milk warm from your cow
When drifted snow kept the milkman away,
With a tin of welshcakes or the hot rice-pudding
Your sister would send us from time to time;
After the day-long roar of your chain-saw
Lopping logs from trunks dumped in your yard
You'd turn up with the wooden wheelbarrow
Full of extra fuel you knew would be welcome.

Both over seventy, your sister and you
Rose around six as you'd done all your lives,
Tended the animals, always kept busy;
From the room where my writing so rarely went well
I watched you both through a long downpour
Tackling fallen trees in the lane,
Stooped to your labours with the barrow and saw.
I felt your easy synonymity
Of life and work reproved my inability
To find a better attitude to my tasks
Behind that window in the copse's shadow.

One April I dug our large garden all week,
Enjoyed the lenience of immediate purpose,
Then admired the rhythms of your expertise
As you cast the soil into even banks,
Sculpting long potato-trenches for us,
The spade lithe in your hands that had polished
Its shaft to hard brightness with years of use.
I recall when you rescued me from incompetence
By conjuring a bean-frame almost in passing
From an intimidating pile of rough sticks and twine;
I wrote about that, never showed it to you,

Who sometimes announced yourself in Welsh,
Confronting me on my own doorstep
With failure to re-possess the language
My childhood heard dwindling in Cardiff
To father's *hiraeth* and mother's *ach y fi.*
Sparing with English, nothing you said to me
Was meant to be memorable, lacking dimensions
Of vigour and rhythm apparent in your Welsh;
Your resonant *diawl* and laughing *boys bach*
Stay as clear as the acts I compose you of now –
Boys bach! How well you loved my sons:

It pleased you that Sam brought *Cymraeg* home from school,
That through his shyness a shift of his eyes
Gave indication that he understood;
They'd pester me to be taken to see you,
To run with grain after your chickens,
To prise the sweets from your teasing clenched fist.
Brought to your dying, they said their 'Goodbye Dic'
Around the door of your hospital room.
I kept away from your cancer, however;
Last time I'd seen you troubled me still,
As part of a past I was trying to distance:

I'd left the old house when the family broke up,
And woke one morning from a blackout-drunk
Unaware that I'd damaged my car, ditched it blocking
Your yard; so you had it repaired, sent a note,
And I came, just thanked you, and drove it away....
Pouring down again, Dic, and dark, though the ripples
Of what the hill drains to the river catch odd gleams
From our lane's single lamp. There you are,
With your wet-weather sack round your shoulders
And the day's last cigarette; there's little to say
As I join you, to smoke, spit, and stare at the rain.

Them

I dream them skating, a diminishing train,
Hands linked from mother through two sizes of young brother,
Surprised to see this on the television news
In the indicative of *freeze*; the camera zooms in close:
Observe my tall ex-consort, leaning into her motion,
Exhibiting a characteristic air
Of disregard, in that fur-trimmed black coat
She's had about ten years; my elder son
Has seen the camera, and looks, it seems, at me
From a pallid face pinched to smallness by grief,
While his little brother stoops to consider
The relationship between his skates and the ice.
They course quite quickly, with adequate confidence,
Across the white expanse. The light is of the dismal sort,
The sublime gloom of a day encompassed
By undifferentiated cloud, whose prolonged resolution
Into millions of tons of snow is imminent.

A lake I knew provides the theme
This frozen one transposes
Into its minor key:
The *locus classicus* of boyhood's perceptions
That my mother is beautiful, when once,
Alone together, she,
In a yellow print dress,
Rowed us across summer water
In a Glasgow park; I recall
Saying little as I looked at her,
The trees on the islands we passed, and the sky,
All intimating some good unity
Of which the eyes sensing no friction
Between their pleasure and any form of *ought*,
And love, and warmth, are aspects.

The dream connotes the arbitrariness
Of memory's invasions of the moment,
Like last month's power-cut seized
By days six years ago with them,
Then us, cohering admirably

Through electricity's absence and snow-drifts' closure.
Though gratefully based in every good provision
Of *home* and all I should wish that to mean,
Sometimes days can't escape the pull
From the neutron star of that collapsed past;
I look down a valley into immeasurable distance
Where desolation of focus fills the actual with emptiness,
In which, perhaps, a high bird is drifting
Like a speck of significance on a blank graph.

Lately, however, passing a northern playing field,
A believer in *the family* might have extended approval
Towards a father and two small sons,
Engrossed at dusk in getting one more flight
From a model aircraft; its recalcitrant engine
Burping at last into a hornet-drone,
The larger scowls with concentration
As he launches it into its tethered gyres;
They gather at the centre, working wires
That make it climb and dive, exhilarated
By this frail construct, its oracle of freedom and connection,
That's circling them at forty miles an hour.

Gently, disintegrating, flesh and the fading *now*
Fall away from the notion of fatherhood;
Going home, this terminated instance
Of our infrequent and too brief reunions
Is settling into memory which emends
The holograph scrawled by the present imperfect
To a version approved for preservation:
Erase sharp irritation at the boys
Trampling appurtenances of model aviation,
Delete the little one's returned 'I don't like you';
Heighten the sweet uniquenesses:
The 'ant-meadow' the younger artificed
From surplus blocks of balsa wood to catch
The ants on sorties round the disused hearth,
Their proof of registering our last meeting
By reference to the church we visited....
Meanwhile, let it be dreams, the chocolate in the post,
Something at Christmas from them,
Photographs, their birth-certificates,
Secreted carefully and proving who they are.

Northampton, 1987

(for Sam and Iggy)

Last Sunday a surreptitious dab of holy water
   On two small foreheads, which surprised you, sons,
My finger dripping from its dip in a receptacle
   That much resembled the bowed ashtrays fixed
To the backs of seats upstairs on the old double-decker buses;
   What's that for Dad? – I'll call it superstition
(Than which 'Irreverance is a greater oaf') to spare me trying
   To detail a theology of how
Quick gratitude keeps outmanoeuvring inert *non serviam*,
   How both *thank* and *defy* must have an object.

It was one of those High Church places where the trappings rise
   To the occasion of the architecture,
All the air below the ceiling's webbed splendour of vaulting
   Succumbing to the sweet oppression of incense,
The priest trussed in his alb smiling the faithful on their way
   As we came in and headed for the transept,
Where works of art, *A.M.D.G.*, by Sutherland and Moore
   Resolved anticipation into attention:
There's Jesus, you said, Ig, approaching the vast cobalt canvas;
   Moore's stone child looked a little bit like you.

Then I went home, a house whose Welsh name means *the sunny hill*,
   Exiled, now voluntarily, from you,
Whose distance is an empty property called *fatherhood*
   That's tenanted on such short holidays;
But to the life I'm glad of here I add more photographs,
   One of you two with Moore's *Madonna and Child*,
Touching its massive base, and touched, perhaps, by the altruism
   Of church and art, a moment in your growing
That you might come across one day, upon which I inscribe
   Though absent please infer me from my loves.

Plas Crug

Love slippery with perspiration
Indoors during the Indian summer
Having gratified the flesh and blood,
Nothing is required beyond this peace
On the equable cemetery's grass,
Though the mouth welcomes the green apple
And idly interferes with silence
Coaxing tunes from a harmonica.

This woman's beauty is *enigma*,
Unfixed as light on a rippling pool:
Ingenuous as the young religieuse,
Lascivious enough for connoisseurs,
She intrigues with indeterminacy,
Implying the physics of deep space
In stellar flashes of teeth and eyes,
Glimpsed moods suggesting the mind's black holes.

The trees are set free as she draws them
Into a wild and fictive landscape,
Redeemed of their municipal function
Of hiding death from the infants school.
Art, though, has no quarrel with endings,
Being all about completed states,
Grave-marble not profaned unduly
By serious hands whose work it supports.

My back respectfully opting for
The blank side of an old slate headstone,
The dead, it is hoped, do not object
To imperfect but sincere renderings
Of 'Ye Banks and Braes O' Bonny Doon'
And other airs of like refinement.
Surrounded by what has to happen
This version of happiness persists.

Pictograph

if I enlarge, I see nothing but the grain…and if I do not enlarge,
if I content myself with scrutinising, I obtain this sole knowledge,
long since possessed at first glance: that this indeed has been.

ROLAND BARTHES,
Camera Lucida

You, in your youth, that has hardly ended,
Wearing only a river from the hips down,
Advance past rippling shallows to a fast pool
Shadowed by abundance of overhanging trees,
Where braided roots and sinewy vegetation
Give the far bank a satyr's musculature.
Over your shoulder you smile at the camera,
Inviting to immersion's cool delight,
Calling me in from nine year's distance,
Where it's December and what you excite
Requires a new tense called the *sexual present*
Expressing how in both kind and degree
My youth and forty years feel this alike.
The confident foliage, the unblemished light
On your nakedness, all acknowledge summer;
By means of powerful lenses, I descend
Through sycamore leaves to grainy generalisations,
And might as well be a bird in this photograph,
Held in my course through its myth of your pleasure,
As here, glimpsing these thin clouds I exhale
But feeling no more cold than you seem to,
My knowing *ingénue*, clasped intimately
By clarities of water, light, and air.
Slipped through the aperture's instant, you become
Discontinuous with your past and future,
Your reflection stilled in its fluid shimmer,
A white encrustation of turbulence fixed
Almost modestly where your full curves submerge.

Weeks pass through which I frequently consider
This image that arrived with marrying you,
Extrapolating only a thin frame
Of random instances that share a landscape:
How once, nine miles upstream and years before,

I too bathed in this river where its thrust
Slows at a deep cleft in lead-bearing rock;
How recently we followed its lowland ogees
Going to renew your friendship with the girl
Whose father's eye behind the viewfinder
Composed my sanctuary against the winter
Where luminous significances congregate.
Transmitting news that thought and flesh accord
Through easy registers of sensation,
Your smile subverts totalitarian cold,
Slips through its cordons policed by stringencies.
The depths of shade and light in all its manners,
From sequin-flicks to elemental white,
Hold focus in your face's chiaroscuro,
That draws me from its record to acknowledge
A present glad to answer for itself.

On the Road

The first lift slipped the sea behind mountains
And the commonsense from behind the wheel
Was admirably modest and well-meant;
The salesman couldn't know his good advice
Was telling the starving to eat plainer food.
At Newtown a youth in a van pulled up;
Not into ethics, he played obscene tapes
By racist comedians in Black Country clubs
Almost to Wolverhampton.

You have to go along with them of course,
Stay shut up with the taciturn, find common ground
In Germany with the ex-soldier driving
A fifteen-tonner stacked with granule-nylon
Bound for extrusion somewhere in Leicestershire,
Which is where you're dropped, and the thumb resumes
Its blatant, ridiculous jerking.

Over there two sons are part of the town
Spread out on a plain as the rig rolls north,
Where the spectacle of pitheads and sunset
Assists in out-manoeuvring feelings
And the miles fall away to the on-song hum
Of sixteen tyres turned east now for the coast.

Days later, a child's wax crayon and cardboard
Make the name of the place that's next on the route.
This is going home; tonight she'll dream
A composite lover that's you and the others
Crossing a derelict warehouse to reach her,
Traversing the final moribund obstacle,
A moaning crone whose bed blocks the gap
In the bricks to the room where sex
Too frankly offered is declined:
An allegory of any pointless journey,
Of going home to have to leave again.

In Progress

Here love is like a long experiment
Observed through changes in the earliest light,
The watcher monitoring his own intent
While pigeons coo and lengthening graphs recite
The weeks spent in the bare laboratory
Away from what he loves till proofs disclose
The bases of his love's integrity,
Its manners, and the thoughts that are its clothes.

Now nothing fills the empty corridors
Except the presence of the others' sleep;
Half-dreaming, half-dispassionate, he bores
Himself by idly wishing he could weep.
In time, but not his own, results will show,
Precipitating out into *I know*.

Judgement

Pausing to spit by prearrangement,
Though without any show of vehemence,
My wives file past my grave, three ladies
Dressed modestly, with dark hair in common,
Along with their claims to having stood
More than a sufficiency of me.
Years back, the taller two departed,
The last I left for this scrubby plot;
My final insult makes this poem
Collect them, who were never gathered
Except in the haphazard sequence
Of acts and avoidances of them
Occurring or not under my name
Between the years printed on that board
My brother spent some time preparing,
Cribbed from his *Book of Celtic Designs.*

My sons come then, with a wheelbarrow
Piled high with wrecked model aircraft;
They tip the oil-soaked balsa debris
On the mound, splash on the methanol,
Then standing well back (as always instructed)
Flick lighted matches till a blue-gold
Whooomph....
                    Befitting my manner of death
When struck by one of my own aircraft,
Wildly erratic on its first flight,
The little pyre smoulders into dusk.

Much as I dislike being so far
From my dictionaries, that told me all
The truth within their grasp (admitting
To grave difficulties with *puzzle*),
The agony of particulars is over.
No differences here to be reconciled
By the straight edge of justification, no frontier
Where impulses are searched for language.
Beyond this, no report is possible;
I sense I'm looking for my father.

Encounter

I met Bruegel in a pub last night
On an ageing Birmingham council estate.
Gone ten o'clock, the drinkers swayed,
Submerged in sentiment, to songs
From a lean young man in a clean white shirt,
Songs they'd known for thirty years,
About love being unattainable, etc.

I had left the room where I live alone
Four nights a week (work away from home),
Walked down the street past the playing field,
And was surprised at the puddled bar
By *The Hunters in the Snow*, not hung
But propped beside bottles, slightly odd
Among bits of wrought iron and synthetic wood.

There we were, Bruegel and I,
On the margins of that society:
Our unloveable *semblables*,
Whom we had to love for their exposition
Of our sad appetites, each skating on
The hour's thin ice, who'd all be gone
At closing time, the hunters in the snow.

Taking a Break

You stand in the yard watching snow fall
In small hard flakes through air starved of light
At eight hundred feet, where there's no one to care
If coal's piled outside the front door.

It's not satisfactory having to love
The darkening afternoon as your twin;
It gives you an eight-year-old death for a present,
The robin you thought you'd rescued from freezing

That twitched to a stillness surviving here
In a day that's just a heartbreaking elegy
For the absence of sex and cash enough
To have something to do when all else fails.

The Butter of Death

Mother, never one to countenance waste,
Wanted the roses from Father's coffin.
He wasn't to be buried for several days,
Said the undertaker after consulting a list,
And showed me out the back way, pointing down
A lane towards a gate where the dead waited.

I walked until I reached a cricket match,
And was reproved for wandering on the pitch;
An elderly spectator gave assistance,
Directed back the way I'd come, and there,
Below the hedge just by the gate, among
The weeds, a brick or two, some rusting iron,
Two caskets lay. It came as a relief,
An easing of my terrible reluctance,
To find Dad's lid unscrewed and him wrapped up
Quite neatly in brown paper, the roses
There for the lifting....

Then Mother decided to hold a wake,
The coffin behind the food and drink
All ranged on the black grand piano;
The party was a great success,
Its life and soul a rather spectral lady
Dressed like Queen Nefertiti.

We ran out of margarine at one point;
I recalled that a tub was in beside Dad,
Was rummaging for it when Mother began
To work on his wrappings with a breadknife,
Cutting lumps like soft icing she eagerly nibbled –
'Here, try this, kid, the butter of death'.

Error Divide Overflow

(for David Attenborough and Geoffrey Hill)

I didn't like it when the monkeys killed
Another monkey of a different kind;
They ripped him up and then they ate their fill.
Somewhere a camera whirred; they didn't mind,

But sat like late Victorians at tea,
Upright in modest dignity and quiet,
Obedient to ordained necessity,
With leaves at hand to supplement their diet.

Their garments of religion, art, and law
Just didn't suit; I saw all history's grief
Extend from slaughter in those boughs that bore
The feasting primates with their perfect teeth.

Outside Beddgelert

i.m. S.H.

The day you died, we'd been balanced on rocks,
Each yard computed to minimise risk,
Working toward the topmost buttresses
Where the sudden level gives space for rest.

Later, the lay-by in flawless daylight,
Pines by the lake, the big motorbike
Losing its grip on the tightening bend;
Missing my sons, it smashed the car sideways
Abrupting a skid's relentless ballistics
In which you totalled only mass-times-speed.

The doctor who stopped couldn't slow your fading
To wood-ash white, gave up, spat out
The blood from your lungs,
So the ambulance men had no more to do
Than spread the tactful red blanket.

The inquest re-united us all:
Your fellow-riders whose 'fuck, oh fuck no...'
Extemporised mourning; the police
Who fixed your shape in yellow chalk
Then measured all the relevant distances....
The pathologist's inventory of your organs
Detached you from those spasms on the tarmac
That ebb to last residual shudders
As my boys come up from the water's edge,
Your passing like the summit's insistence
That there is no more beyond its emptiness,
Your gift to them of the knowledge of death.

North Road

Through glass rain blurs a long look down
Across the town to where the sea
Becomes distinct from mist and night
In white explosions on the quay
And crests the gale breaks in the bay.

Downstairs the repetitious years
Elide with caring's piety
The gap between old age and death;
What happens happens quietly,
Like the concentric vanishing O's

Big drops make in the puddled yard,
Surfeits of zeroes arguing
Tautologies of nullity.
While some keep faith that everything
Encodes a reason we can't read,

Upstairs the psychiatric ward's
For those who've gone past thinking straight;
The syrups, pills, and ECT
Encourage symptoms to abate,
Success rates qualified by some

Who wouldn't wait to be discharged
Before they bid for suicide
As the least pointless strategy
For countering the steady tide
Of days whose terms they couldn't take.

A visit done to one who tried,
We leave her in her well-lit room,
Content, it seems, she failed to drain
The veins she slashed, set to resume
Negotiations with her life.

A Visit to the Library

Since my last visit and the poet-librarian's death
  The place had changed beyond recognition:
A darkness almost palpable seemed to emanate
  From the panelling and the central staircase,
Black with ancient varnish crazed like crocodile skin.
  Behind a balustrade at the stairhead
A sublibrarian-priest held up the bright brass sphere
  Encasing the poet-librarian's skull
And, rubbing it, set up a throbbing resonance
  That mounted to a blizzard of a moan:
It paralysed the will with fear and indecision,
  Then faded into echoing recessions.
I ran upstairs and found a passage to a tower,
  From which he leapt, his crimson cape a sail.
I took the spiral steps, emerging through an arch
  To sunlight on a seventeenth century green
Where King Charles II stood by a four-poster;
  He said the cracked and blackened corpse it bore
Was Merexant, the poet and executed traitor,
  A transmigrationist whose brazen orb,
He'd claimed, had housed his soul before and would again.
  Once I got home this troubled me for weeks,
Till days anaesthetised by snow forced apperception
  To stare into the bleak weather of self
As at a single tree in the monochrome landscape;
  I at last derive a cold serenity
From pondering the long perspectives of succession.

Time and Flight: An Afterword

(for Walter Wood and Nev Dickenson)

Many ingenious lovely things are gone
W.B. YEATS.

It is a death, this riven devastation
Brute impact shocked throughout a shape that flew
With power and grace in aquiline equation;
Its form's returned to where all forms are new,
The place before the plan, whence Euclid's lines
And dreams of flight across millenia
Emerge into this realm where time confines
All artefacts in thrall to matter's mania
For imperfection, breakage, and decay.
Mere days into its aerobatic prime
This aircraft proves what Yeats's poems say:
'Things fall apart', 'no enemy but time';
Connections fail, functions disintegrate,
In myths, societies, and model 'planes,
So on the last swoop out of a square-eight
An instant plunge annulled the builder's pains
With satin balsa, measurement, blades, glue:
Beyond a curse's use, the sky-blue wreck
Lies strewn, its costly motor hid from view,
Rammed through municipal turf till hands effect
An excavation. Stuff the lot away
To drip exhaust-oil down its splintered frame
Till salvaging odd bits helps to defray
Expenses for another of the same,
If luck and judgement can contrive to match
Its excellences: this was a machine
That for the first time licensed me to snatch
Prerogatives of flight as sure and clean
As those that mark the 'planes the experts fly,
Which do not stagger, overweight, round turns
But with a rigorous elegance cleave the sky.
O thing of beauty, now thy pilot learns,
Too late, the need to check each crucial yoke
On which the polity of control depends,
For when the motor with its thundering stroke
Thrusts through the ether its propeller rends

The gods of flight don't tolerate the crime
Of carelessness....And now please tell my wife
I'm in the shed and might be quite some time
With virgin wood and well-honed modelling knife.

Tramontane

It is a play no rationalist would write
JOHN TRIPP

Within the glassed box of the bus-shelter
A youth whose head is bowed, whose lower lip droops
With difficulty or absorption, over what he reads,
Stares at an introductory page signed
In facsimile by its one-book author,
Whose spikily legible hand reveals
Mein Kampf (in English) still commands attention.
Its regrettably credible thesis,
Syllogistically pairing man and beast,
Persists in consequences of its consequences
Beside the harbour. While mast-pulleys rattle
In November wind that makes the rigging wires sing,
The proprietor of the town's best restaurant
Becomes once more what he'd rather not be,
A displaced German drunk whose lopsided smile
Attempts the maintenance of appearances
While, awash with self-pity and *Gerwürztraminer*,
He explains himself to the fixtures and fittings,
Emotively reiterating *Stalingrad*, *Stalingrad*,
Sechste Armee, mein Vater ist in Stalingrad gefallen…
His chef has heard it all before, supposes
He'll pull himself together by this evening
When leaders of a political committee
Will dine there with their party's *Wunderkind*,
The Right Honourable Member for Ponsley Mongford,
Whose 'Forward in Strength' speech has boosted morale
Throughout the nation, brought him to such places as this.
The absence of a stalwart of long standing,
The Chairman of the local British Legion,
Whose lungs that filled with oil in '41
Gave up while he was out of town on holiday,
Will tone the jollity down while he's remembered;
His coffin is detraining as the *Journal*,
Which takes municipal pride in his obituary,
Is dumped in bundles at the station news-stand.
Only dispersing vapour trails detract

From the sky's blue perfection of emptiness
Above ornate frontages of old brick
That rich light reddens to their nature as baked earth
While smooth wheels bear the body on its penultimate stage
Towards a small cemetery on a steep incline
Where spirit-level and plumb-bob contrive
A regimented neatness that's impressive from a distance.
The barber opposite the taxi-rank
Glimpses the hearse departing in his mirror,
Knows who it is, recalls the old boy's trims
And their agreement in baffled disaffection
With the government they'd both helped to elect.
He's casting a more neutral vote next time,
He informs his customer's reflection
In the immediate foreground of the glass;
The conversation moves on to guest-houses,
Unhurried scissors ceasing for point-making pauses
During which his eyes fix those in the mirror
With practised earnestness that's disconcerting
In one whose skills are paid for to cut hair.

The light fades and the tide is coming in
When the man who hopes to be next summer's sensation
As 'Wales's Greatest Sand-Sculptor' abandons
The Last Supper (his ninth, improved, attempt)
To dissolution and a shivering German
Who, having tried to buy it, pressed ten pounds in his hand
Because it was *wunderschön*, *wunderschön*.
Far out at sea the horizon's distorting lens
Gently squeezes the blood-orange sun out of sight
As the surf begins carving sharp concavities
In the tableau's base. The restaurateur cries a little,
Then continues the walking the breathing of ozone,
That will leave him feeling more or less sober,
And *shrecklich*, but ready, he thinks, for the booking,
With their guest and their money from beyond the mountains.

To the Benton Soviet, Newcastle

(for Sean O'Brien)

> *What way will you...mature its mutandum and*
> *bring it ultimately to passable factivity?*
> MARTIN FINNUCANE

Excitement of your visit subsides
To nine-syllable monotonies:
The fog that could be sold in cling-film,
The quadruple scotch, the dead-pan hills
Where ferns collapse in sodden tangles,
Our people dyslexic as ever
Faced with the bold print of normalcy.
O how we love to entertain you –
Guest emissaries of small states like ours,
Whose sole resource is the alphabet,
Whose enormous moral stamina
And unreasonable behaviour
Are ever assured of a welcome
By our confirmed irresolution
And unreasonable behaviour.

We regret our Boeotia affords
No apter idiom to address you,
Who ornament our very language,
Whose Lit. and Phil.'s ideal we envy,
So keen to credit your industry
With every due of prodigiousness;
We rejoice in similarity
Of effort and intention, knowing
That only such polities as ours
Insist upon the leader making verses
As the first condition of office,
The lexis and its implications
His nemesis and life abundant.

– The People's Republic of Melindwr, Year 5.

Taliesin: Interim Report

(for Jaroslaw Kosciuszko)

> *I am Taliesin. I sing perfect metre,*
> *Which will last to the end of the world.*

No big men now whose mountainside camp-fires
Glimpsed from the bay hushed sea-going mendicants,
Who for my verses fat with flattery
Saw me all right for wine and bagged gold,
From whose superfluities of women and horses
I made my selections and left.
Power dripped from those wilds slowly, squeezed
By the long closure of armies, dogma;
Then centuries, successively more chancy –
Killed in a pub in Deptford that time,
Called mad or treacherous, saint or drunkard,
Increasingly prone to such miscalculations
As my verbal elixirs lost efficacy
To charm my ample perquisites from fortunes
Glittering their transits down the generations.

Like a well outside an expired village
I shed my usefulness, stared blankly skyward,
And, bound to language, was spouse to silence
When money assumed a god's taciturnity.
I survived Victoria as an ivied headstone
Incised with twenty of Milton's syllables –
But O the heavy change, now thou art gone,
Now thou art gone, and never must return.
The wars got ridiculous: five hundred pounds
Of high explosive by air from Krefeld
Blew me back into the routine of birth.

It took me thirty years to find the chieftains,
Bored at the ends of their heavy oak tables,
Amusing themselves with numerical riddles
They try to solve by juggling variables
Of unit costs and fealty of workers.
I sing their processes, breathe life into their products,
I glorify them in the halls of their reports;
Their gratitude for perfect punctuation,
For my priesthood of the unsplit infinitive,

And sweet modalities veiling persuasions,
Is shown in the miniature poems they make
Of my name and some figures on slips of stiff paper,
Admitting me to deference, worlds of choice.

THE BOOK OF SHACKLETON

Les Très Riches Heures du Shackleton

(for Jenny Stringer)

Shackleton breakfasts, discarding sleep's relics,
Mostly amorphous, some rather troubling;
Snow falling heavily, air grey and windless,
Shackleton staring, drifting away.

Shackleton gathers his papers, his list
Of names that his reading will turn into people,
Opens his folder at table eleven,
Works through till tea in the basement-canteen;

Shackleton likes his misanthropy silenced
By talk with the Keeper of Printed Books,
Wonders if God would intrude on his atheism,
Flattering Shackleton out of routine.

Shackleton exiting through a succession
Of doors, always pleased at outside's mild surprise;
Shackleton's dinner, Shackleton clicking
The switch for the gas to keep Shackleton warm.

Shackleton pulling away from reluctance
Out to the current he usually finds,
Borne now through pages Shackleton's writing,
Better than watching the war on TV.

Shackleton's breather, peeing where mice rot
Out in the yard in curdling mist;
Shackleton's rule of thumb before sleeping,
Measuring the day, finding it fits.

Shackleton's Inadvertency

The police closed in on him, mercifully, mercifully,
As he sat at the wheel, blankness vibrating
Through synapses shocked at the impact produced
When the pier so abruptly embraced his car.
The sea was detachment, endlessly, endlessly
Shifting behind the 'Come along now',
Uttered with sternness, not without kindness,
By a ruddy young face that winced at his breath.
Professionally patient, the desk-sergeant helped with
The questions that seemed inappropriately factual,
Filled in the forms, impounded his licence,
Called for another to lead him downstairs;
Hours confined with the smell of disinfectant,
Hangover edging in, deepening, broadening,
Prospect of limitless shame and regret.
Good Dr Shackleton, why can't you manage,
Grievously missing your *Kinder und Frau*,
Is it the whisky or merely existence
Making you kneel at the lavatory now?
Mercifully, mercifully, days on, subsiding
To the mild inconvenience of travelling by bus
To and from counselling, group therapy sessions,
Shackleton taking the future on trust.

Shackleton's Magnum Opus

of making many books there is no end
ECCLESIASTES

In bibliographical panic he's searching
Through catalogue cards lined along the equator,
Friable wafers his fingers are crumbling
In their hurry to trace a fugitive work.
He runs from the library to cancel the reference,
Then remembers his son, who waits to be taken
To the County Asylum; as they go, he sings

His favourite hymn, to 'Bid my anxious fears subside'.
Further delay in Bolton, embroiled
With John Wesley in a buffeting mob
Hired by the local incumbent;
Delivered with scratches, Wesley directs him
Along the road to the Derbyshire Peak,
Where he finds his bundle of eight hundred pages
Beneath a hedge in incessant hail,
Shackleton's Dictionary of Weathers dissolving,
Making a joke of the deadline's abyss.
With the *Meisterwerk* in a black plastic sack,
He descends towards some fields in the distance
Where the better weather seems to begin.

Shackleton and the Important Man

Only the dreamer venoms all his days,
Bearing more woe than all his sins deserve
JOHN KEATS

Weeks in the maze of the underground stacks
Alone with two hundred years' magazines
Have exposed him too much to the rarified dust
From pages uncut since Victorian print-shops.
Time goes slack on him, lost between deadlines
At six-pence a word in permanent dusk,
Finds he's the White Knight explaining to Alice
How consciousness causes such desolation,
Postponing the proof of his Theory of String.

Waking's a struggle, mephitic emissions
From negative depths of his bank account
Forming a noxious deposit on morning
That's rinsed off with dousings of coffee by ten.

Night and he's tramping uphill in drizzle,
Spongy turf, rushes, the moon intermittent
On bog-cotton nebulae in clammy darkness,
Heading to meet the Important Man.
Fallen in peat-slime up to his elbows,

Bleeding from impact of knuckles on quartz,
Past desperation, the hovel admits him
To silences stretching between brief non-sequiturs
Issuing from the Important Man.

Dimness infected with peat-smoke and cat-piss,
Shackleton weary, the Important Man
Not quite ignoring his suffering presence,
Shrewdly dismantling a large apparatus,

Easing the cataract of ratiocination,
Opening a space where the pair of them sit.
'There is a lizard in your stomach' –
The Important Man stirs a green preparation,
Shackleton drinking, gagging, swallowing,
Rising in thirty seconds to stagger,
Sightless, vertiginous, vomiting over
A chipped enamel bowl into which
The Important Man is slipping a lizard:

Shackleton in focus, groaning, recoiling,
Parts with a tenner, haste unconcealed,
Makes his way back through fresh air to the stacks
Where Alice attends a tangle of string.

Shackleton's Despair

'When I count, there are only you and I together'
T.S. ELIOT
The Waste Land

It comes to him like an old friend
Whose convictions concerning being alive
Are the perma-frost on his expression.
They sit there watching television,
Which purveys competing apologias
For failures of justice, love, economics.

The face settles into its dead-pan consonance
With certain naturally occurring austerities:

Rock that knows there's nothing for it
But to wait till water's done its job;
Grey seas weary in their assurance
That Nietzsche was right and it goes on forever.

The redeemer, amusement, has a half-hearted go
At feeding the five thousand fears with a laugh
But there's not so much as a literary titter
And the wind says 'piss off' as it beats up the rain.

Shackleton's Interludes

Leaving infancy is glimpsed
Chiefly in terms of a figure remembered,
The context obscure, but no less a city,
Big dirty buildings, December, snow –
He must have been representing God,
And his beard, a white synthetic fleece,
Shone in the light from the fireworks
As he smiled down from the wide balcony.

Forty years on the prospect of Christmas
Was gaudy, pathetic, the ten-thirty reflex
Letting the alcohol into his blood,
Enough to soften, or a little more.
His notion from staring at the white table
Became that he'd die and find himself
Arrived to discover the balcony empty,
Then feel the earthquake that would pull it down.

A white cat at ease between moves
Among shrubbery where mist isolates
A well-tended garden out on a hillside.
At this he feels unaccountably happy,
Imagines the breeze neglecting the mist,
The flags limp down on the promenade,
December wearing its misery
As the closest fitting of all ancient habits.

Returned, he said he'd seen the Great Sunset
On leaving the library, its bronze doors open
On indigo islands setting perspectives
Deep into orange fire above the sea.
The moment attention slipped from that light
He thought of terror and love's modest clumsiness,
Though neither troubled him as much
As the sudden, lost, connection he'd made.

Shackleton in the Capital

He can no longer understand the city,
Where every surface shimmers with July;
Its eloquence is plain, a superfluity
Of mobile meanings joined tangentially,
But all its rhythms slip sideways from the point
At which he tries commencing apprehension:
The glaring murderess multiplied in print
Needs day-glo hair to guarantee attention.
The watts increase, the continuities slacken,
And air-conditioning proliferates;
He looks ahead and sees regression quicken,
The fifties drive past in a white estate,
And lets his chilled beer counteract dismay,
Become a glass set where his eyelids shut
Out sunlight on the *Promenade des Anglais*:
The tiny blisters of appearing sweat
Are swelling to spill runnels down his brow
Though usage hasn't grown arthritic yet
And cuts its capers on the spume of *now*.
Moves on, sleeps near the zoo, gets up to find
The day a crossword he's left incomplete,
Nagged by the gap from *misery* to *condign*;
Thought of *the nicest man you'd hope to meet*,
Juggling such cliches till he reached the door
That Engels used for telling *out* from *in*
From 1870 to '94,
Crossed to the pub, sat outside with a gin.

Somewhat divided when considering style,
He ticked *yes* often on the questionnaire,
Concluded it was pleasant for a while,
By noon was navigating out of there.

Shackleton Takes a Break

Dread where dusk is closing down the world
To the black encirclement of peaks,
Snow grudgingly lodged in high gullies,
The cold refining desolation.

He fades into this, stands hitchhiking
Where there's no traffic, amused earlier
To ride north with three tons of sheeps' guts
In black polypropylene barrels.

He sees his intentions perching on twigs,
Queries their wish for his solitude
Amid the rock's gothic narcosis
Where being human's inappropriate.

By the time he reaches seven men
Crouched at noon in a shallow cave
All summits have been cancelled,
All waterproof clothing is sodden.

The plating of ice drips from the boulders,
The lichen is bloated, treacherous, greasy.
This is a day that ends at lunchtime
With the gale snatching the meat from the sandwich.

He will compare it later with another
Encountered in sunlight on a flat street
Where the front door closes like a submarine diving
To austerities below the surface of choice.

Shackleton et Fils

Out on the empty beach he plays with verse
Much as his infant son does with the sand,
Observes that here his mood seems to expand
Till rhythm's buoyancy dispels the curse
And parodies of Wordsworth intersperse
The silences between events that stand
Autonomous as purposes disband;
The day's a blank where language may rehearse
Its tendencies to organise round sound,
Extravagant and aureate, facile, flowing,
Uttered and lost with no one to confound
This talent the unconscious is bestowing
In sweet encounters with the air around
A beach they like and leave with nothing owing.

Shackleton's Love Song

Come with me to a caravan
On a hill above the bay,
The rain it raineth all it can
From June right through till May.

We'll live on beans and cheap corned beef,
Drink cider, *quant. suff.* plus,
You'll be a whore and I a thief,
O how they'll envy us.

* * *

Poet Laureate Ritual Bath Murder

Big Ted's coming for you, lad,
He's outside the bathroom door.
He's tall and dark and he's strong and mad
And he's not from Elsinore.

When your head goes under the water
To rinse away the shampoo
That's Ted, that cold on your dripping back,
And he knows what he's got to do.

He'll explain before he kills you
About the Egyptian tomb,
How Anubis flattens the corn-circles,
While his eyes' deep mineral gloom

Starts glowing when he gets to
The thought that suddenly flashed
When you read a book about Mithraism
The last time you got smashed.

The bath's gone cold as he gets out
The curving silver knife
And when he's done he'll go downstairs
And do things with your wife.

Sweeney in Senectute

Excuse me, they don't all get pinched in the end.
T.S. ELIOT
'Fragment of an Agon'

Henceforth old age, a time from whence
What the obituarist can't know –
An awful daring in a room
Demolished, maybe, years ago –

Stabs at him with its point of fact
And leers from Paris, 1910,
When she, to please for twenty francs,
Persuaded him to try again.

After the first time he'd slipped out
Into a bleak and sickening dream –
He watched six badgers masturbate
In a streetlight's yellow gleam.

I knew a man once did a girl in.
Any man might do a girl in
Any man has to, needs to, wants to
Once in a lifetime, do a girl in

She wouldn't stop, her sweat, her flesh,
Were suffocating sanity;
Back on the street his fear advised
'Resume your chill urbanity'.

Such knowledge, what forgiveness then?
No answer came next afternoon,
The ferry's slowly lengthening wake
Blank as the dark side of the moon,

And forty years of prayer do not
Make matters of such import clearer,
Anxiety increasing as
The lean solicitor draws nearer.

W.B. Yeats in LSD Horror

The pill was green and flecked with black
Like Connemara marble,
The dealer a stoned Dublin boy
With the usual spiel to garble –

He drew my attention to the Secret Rose
With which each tab was stamped,
Blathered a bit about *purity man*,
Took a fiver and then decamped.

I was sitting on a bench in Stephen's Green
When the city began to change –
I felt like the Wind Among the Reeds
Was breezing through my veins;

The trees were lush-leafed armadillos
Each the size of Ben Bulben's Head,
And the sky after flashing green and mauve
Was the Rose of the World that bled

Till the blood-dimmed tide swept me into night
To the foot of a tall square tower
Where a man in a grey cape on the roof
Called down 'It is the hour;

Phase twenty-eight, the Gyres! the Gyres!
Come forth; we await your word',
Then flapping his cape he twitched a bit
And turned into a golden bird.

The darkness slipped, coagulated
To a vast rotating cone
And we flew through the racial memory
Till I found myself alone

In a library of ten million shelves
Beyond the edge of space
And every book was by or about
The late William Butler Yeats.

Designer-hell for acid-heads
With a daft obsession for verse!
I took the *Collected Poems* down
And read about Cromwell's Curse.

O what of that, O what of that,
What is there left to say?
While the gale howled through the ruin of time
That was neither night nor day.

In the *Stella Matutina*
The hot-stuff seemed to lurk
And I found the Latin phrases
That lit the fireworks –

The very air was hopping
With caballistic signs
And Yeats jumped out of the woodwork
Screaming 'The Great Design...

The bobbin's broken, now the loom
Whose weaving I inspire
To pattern out the coming age
Collapses in the mire.'

He started shaking, cracks appeared
In the stiff folds of his face
And a heaving set up through the floor
As vibrations wrecked the place.

O dark, dark, dark as I sped out
Beyond the exploding Yeats,
Who flickered out his half-life
Through the interstellar states.

Dawn breaking over Stephen's Green,
I let reality in,
And the golden bird in my pocket
Turned out to be made of tin.

Campaign

(for Lyn Hejinian)

We are not certain what it is we seek,
Nor if by going forward we advance.
Our plans are kept alive from week to week.

We hear the trees but would not say they speak;
Although their theme remains 'Autumnal Chance',
We are not certain what it is we seek.

Each blink and twitch prolongs this losing streak
Where indecision holds us in a trance.
Our plans are kept alive from week to week.

Our plausibility has sprung a leak,
The ladies don't give us a second glance.
We are not certain what it is we seek.

It's how you're facing when you're up the creek
That calls the tune to which you have to dance.
Our plans are kept alive from week to week.

The vicar sighs 'Life's got a bloody cheek'
Then sleeps to dream he's dining out in France.
We are not certain what it is we seek.
Our plans are kept alive from week to week.

Nicotinic Sonnet

I like it when I feel the tingle spread
Down through the legs, the blood bearing the news
That smoke is passing down the bronchial flues,
That someone lied who called the habit dead.
The will steps down, its credibility shed;
Something's got what it wants, will have its dues
In wheezing, yellowed fingers, other clues
To what's beyond the thickening smoke ahead.
The packet's empty now, I'll try again,
Though there's a stress crack through what I intend
Whence craving pleads *Let smoking take the strain;*
While you can lift a hand a fag's your friend,
A point of reference on the darkling plain,
Abstain from abstinence until the end.

On the Knocker

They are not to blame, the rich,
For much that troubles me.
Their wonderfully fitted crazy paving,
Dead straight and eight feet wide
Down to their tall front doors,
Is a mode of delight set off by lawns
That level their green symmetries at noon.
They have, as a rule, very little to do
With ugliness and disorder.
Their carpets, whose assuaging depths
Buoy up such pale unblemished hues,
Are not of this world and wholly remote
From pavements disfigured with weeping or vomit.
They display a commendable interest in art
And prize their paid-up connoisseurship
Above many excellent acquisitions.
The rich, unlike myself,
Are not consumed with reasonable envies.
The TV does not tout what they may lack.
Their finely wrought antipathies
Are not the predictable pits in response
Politeness skirts when talking to the poor.
They ornament equality when friendly,
Though I distrust the pleasure this provokes;
Simpler to discount the quick dismissal
Electronically rasped through a grille
After submitting to inspection
By the fish-eye lens discreetly tucked
In the masonry of a commodious porch.
When the night's a mess and November's dying
They may regret how seldom they must make
Those sad concessions to necessity
Mapping the limits others must inhabit.